CAMPFIRE COOKBOOK

---

50 EASY & YUMMY RECIPES FOR BEGINNERS PERFECT FOR COOKING OUTDOOR

JORDAN WOOD

2

information presented, whether for breach of contract, tort, negligence, personal injury, criminal intent, or under any other cause of action.

You agree to accept all risks of using the information presented inside this book.

You agree that by continuing to read this book, where appropriate and/or necessary, you shall consult a professional (including but not limited to your doctor, attorney, or financial advisor or such other advisor as needed) before using any of the suggested remedies, techniques, or information in this book.

4

Table of Contents

Introduction 9

Breakfast 13

   Banana Bread Pancakes 13

   Perfect French Toast 15

   Avocado Toast Breakfast Sandwich 17

   Sausage Sandwich with Honey Sriracha Sauce 19

   Chickpea Breakfast Hash with Veggies 21

   Banana Coconut French Toast 23

   Turmeric Tofu Scramble 25

   Coconut Chocolate Granola 27

Poultry 30

   Chicken Meatballs and Pasta 30

   One Pot Chicken Rigatoni 32

   Rice With Chicken & Chorizo 34

   Chicken and Squash One-Pot Meal 37

   Cheesy Baked Chicken Spaghetti Casserole 39

   Chicken Stew a la Bonne Femme 41

   Chicken Divan 43

Meat 46

   Apple Cheddar Burgers with Caramelized Onions 46

   Big Ol' Breakfast Burrito 48

   Campfire Stuffed Peppers 50

Classic Beef Kabobs 52

Campfire Cajun Sausage and Pepper Foil Packs 54

Texas BBQ Bloody Mary 56

Lights Frito Pie 58

Seafood *61*

Lime-Drizzled Fish Tacos 61

Orange Bacon Salmon Skewers 63

Grilled Shrimp and Mushrooms 65

Ying and Yang Salmon 67

Tequila Jalapeño Scallops 69

Grilled Snapper 70

Swordfish Steak Skewers 71

Vegetables *73*

Tofu Skewers with Spicy Peanut Sauce 73

Marinated Mushroom Kabobs 75

Creamy Grilled Potato Salad 77

Balsamic Glazed Veggie Kabobs 79

Potato Salad with Bacon Vinaigrette 81

Artichokes with Harissa-Honey Dip 83

Cumin Chili Potato Wedges 85

Soups *87*

Thai Curry Pumpkin Soup 87

Italian Tomato and Orzo Soup 88

Bread Soup with Greens...90

Butternut Squash and White Bean Stew...................................92

Green Chile And Corn Chowder 94

Fish Stew with Tomatoes 96

Spiced Chickpea and Potato Stew..97

Desserts *100*

Brown Sugar Berry Crisp 100

Gooey Caramel Baked Apples... 102

Nutty Salted Caramel Popcorn 104

Quick And Easy Peach Pie 106

Pineapple Upside-Down Cake 108

Buttermilk Chocolate Cake 110

Double-Chocolate Brownies 112

Conclusion.. *115*

Introduction

What are the outdoor cooking hacks that you can be following in your kitchen? You might eat a lot of food in your kitchen. But you don't have to go through the tedious process of cooking. You can let some of the Dutch oven to do the job for you. But it will require a lot of efforts from your side. Following are some of the outdoor cooking hacks that you can go through in the long run. These hacks will help you to save your time and effort too. A lot of Dutch oven usually yields a lot of benefits to the people.

If you want something that is safer than the wood-burning stove, you should have such a gas cooker. You will be using gas instead of firewood in a wood stove. You will be assured of complete safety from heat. You can also have a different cooking taste which will taste amazing. You will be able to cook also your vegetables thoroughly which will give you the best flavor. You can serve someone from the outdoors. It is considered as a part of your house. You will have something that your family might need from time to time. You will be able to ask for a better taste of food.

You can make a single meal and serve it in the outdoors. It will give you a taste that is better than the food you are used to. In India, a lot of people have made outdoor cooking possible because there will be different approaches. It will compare to the indoors on how it is made and how it tastes. In India, there are different indoor and outdoor cooking utensils available. A person might get confused with his choice also. You should just choose the cooking device that will suit your budget. There are different brands available nowadays. It will not give you more financial pressures. You can go for a small budget as well. It will be an easy and simple decision for you to make. It will go for the same amount as of using an indoor gas area kitchen. You will be able to serve a lesser quantity of food. It will save a lot of money for the buyer. It will give you the freedom to improve your cooking style. You can come up with better cooking way in spite of any building or compound. You will be able to serve delicious dinner all the time. It will save your time and energy too. It will help you in social improvement as well. You can serve your guest or others too. It will give them a healthier and tastier food.

You can be able to improve your culinary skills. You will be able to experience something that is worth to taste. One could analyze that you will be totally free from firewood. It will save the environment from pollution as well. You will be able to feel better in the future. You will be able to start your own food business. You will be able to be creative in your own way in cooking. You will be able to earn the extra money to spend the extra money. But you will still be able to manage your budget to a better extent. You will not have a lot of problems in the longer range. It will help you to improve the food business in your country or in the region. If you are looking for something that will prove helpful in the money department, you should try like this. You can find a lot of benefits with several outdoor cooking hacks. It will help you in an affordable way. You will not have a lot of budget issues. In a lot of countries, it will help you to change your lifestyle. You will have a complete package of outdoor cooking. It will be sufficient for your home cooking of different things.

You will end up spending lesser cash for the outdoor cooking. It will contribute to your finances for further use. You can also promote these ideas in order to escalate the cookers. You can share these ideas with your friends and family. You should try to go for a better quality product. You can keep in mind the quality that you need to have. You will not have to worry about your friend or friend who has a different cooking experience. You should definitely try this one out. You can get the benefit of experimenting with it. You will be able to understand how much work you need to put towards this outdoor cooker. It can become a hobby for you in the days to come. You can involve with this outdoor cooking without any problem and issue. You will be able to perform better in your personal life. It will help you with the better skills. You can be creative with the dishes you are preparing. It will help you a lot in the long run. You can start with a small stove and an electric cord. It will give you a feel of an outdoor cooker. You can definitely try this one out and get the optimum benefits in the long run. It is very useful for your different kinds of cooking modes. It will go with your different cooking techniques. It will help you in your outdoor cooking experiments. You can definitely have your outdoor experiments cooking without any problem.

You can enjoy yourself with your friends and family. It will improve your cooking skills. It will give you an outdoor cooking experience. You will have a lot of fun altogether. In India, it will change your lifestyle. You can start a food business with your friends. You will not have any problem in starting a food business. You can go for the first three days and make a good amount of money. You can also consider doing anything outdoors. In the outdoors, you can make different recipes. You will have plenty of good opportunities in life.

You will not have the best results in the beginning. You can be careful and make the best of your situation. You should definitely consider a product that is useful in lots of ways. You will be able to improve your cooking skills. You will enjoy a lot altogether. You will be able to enjoy a much better life. It will help you to make the best of your outdoor cooking experiences. It will be a place for the cooking experiments in short run. You will be able to explore different ideas about cooking. You will be able to have control over your dishes. It will be better to try out this outdoor cooking experience. You will be able to contribute to the needy people in the surrounding areas. It will benefit you in many ways.

Breakfast

Banana Bread Pancakes

Preparation Time: 15 minutes

Cooking Time: 6 minutes

Servings: 16

Ingredients:

- 3 bananas
- 2 eggs
- 1 & 1/2 cup of whole milk
- 2 cups flour
- 1/4 cup of brown sugar
- 2 tsp of cinnamon
- 2 teaspoons of baking powder

- 1 teaspoon of salt
- 1 cup sliced walnuts (toasted if needed in a dry skillet)
- A pan for ghee, butter, or coconut oil

Directions:

In a medium bowl, put two bananas and mash thoroughly until moderately smooth with the back of a fork. Cram the egg in a mixture and add this to the milk. Beat together the banana, the egg, and the milk until creamy.

Add the dry fixings to the bowl and blend with the wet ingredients until well mixed. You should add an optional 1/4 cup of milk if the batter is too thick.

Over medium-low to medium heat, place a nonstick pan or well-seasoned stainless-steel skillet on your burner.

To coat the plate, add a gentle dab of ghee, butter, or coconut oil and swirl. Onto the middle of the skillet, add 1/3 cup pancake batter and disperse some of the sliced walnuts on top.

Cook before the top starts to bubble for a few minutes, and the sides are set (2-3 minutes). Flip the pancake using a spatula and cook the other side until crispy.

For each pancake, repeat for the rest of the batter, adding more ghee or oil as required to the plate. Stack the pancakes and line them with maple syrup or butter, sliced banana, and extra toasted walnuts for serving. Enjoy.

Nutrition:

Calories 152; Carbohydrates 9 g; Protein 8g; Fat 12g

Perfect French Toast

Preparation Time: 15 minutes

Cooking Time: 10 minutes

Servings: 8

Ingredients:

- 1/2 lb. loaf of bread
- 2 Eggs
- 1 cup of milk
- 1 tsp of butter, and plenty to scatter

- 1 teaspoon of cinnamon
- 1 teaspoon extract of vanilla, optional
- 1/4 teaspoon of nutmeg, optional
- 2 tablespoons of butter for pan
- Top Maple Syrup & Berries

Directions:

Cut the bread into slices 3/4-1" "thick. First, beat the eggs in a big enough bowl to fit a slice of the bread.

Then mix milk, cinnamon, nutmeg, vanilla, and sugar, until thoroughly blended. Heat 4 teaspoons of butter over medium heat in a pan.

In the egg and milk mixture, dip a slice of bread and let it soak on each side for around 10 seconds. Let the excess trickle off, sprinkle additional sugar on each side, and then fry it on each side, approximately 3 minutes per side, in the skillet once it gets golden and crispy.

Repeat with the remainder loaf, adding more butter if required to the skillet. Serve with maple syrup, fruit, and a hot coffee cup. Enjoy.

Nutrition:

Calories 275

Carbohydrates 125g

Proteins 75g

Fat 89g

Avocado Toast Breakfast Sandwich

Preparation Time: 15 minutes

Cooking Time: 15 minutes

Servings: 1

Ingredients:

- 2 Bacon slices, sliced in half
- 2 Bread slices
- 1 egg
- 1 avocado
- Salt + pepper

Optional: a pinch of everything but the seasoning of the bagel

Directions:

Set your campfire or camp stove with a cast-iron skillet over it. Put the bacon in the skillet, then cook until crispy over medium-low heat, flipping periodically. Remove and place on a plate lined with a paper towel.

Toast or fry the bread in the pan, rotating so that all sides are browned after about a minute. Simply remove and set aside. Put a bit more fat to the skillet if required. Crack the pan with an egg and prepare it to your taste.

Slice the avocado in half to assemble the sandwich, squirt out the center, and apply it on both slices of bread. Layer on one side the bacon, on the other side the egg, and season with salt plus pepper.

Nutrition:

Calories 103

Carbohydrates 8g

Proteins 7g

Fat 5g

Sausage Sandwich with Honey Sriracha Sauce

Preparation Time: 15 minutes

Cooking Time: 6 minutes

Servings: 6

Ingredients:

- Sausage Patties:
- 1 pound of ground pork
- Dried herbs, around 2 teaspoons: thyme, rosemary, sage, etc.
- 1 teaspoon of salt

- Sriracha Honey Sauce:
- 1/2 cup of honey
- 1 tablespoon of Sriracha
- Assemble the Sandwich:
- Eggs
- Slices of cheese
- Breakfast muffins / English muffins

Directions:

For the sausages, combine the ground pork, herbs, and salt in a broad bowl until thoroughly mixed. Morph into 6 patties of similar percentage, bearing in mind that they can shrink slightly when cooking.

For the sauce, mix the honey and Sriracha in a small bowl, then whisk. Then set aside.

Over the campfire or stovetop, heat a griddle or skillet. Place the sausages on the surface until heated, then cook until browned for 2-3 minutes.

Flip and cook until browned on the other hand for another 2-3 minutes. Meanwhile, as needed, cook the eggs and toast the English muffins.

Spread on the English muffins the Sriracha honey sauce, then layer with a sausage patty, egg, and cheese slice. Serve and enjoy.

Nutrition:

Calories 600; Carbohydrates 12g; Proteins 19g; Fat 35g

Chickpea Breakfast Hash with Veggies

Preparation Time: 15 minutes

Cooking Time: 20 minutes

Servings: 2

Ingredients:

- 1 tablespoon of oil
- 1 summer squash or zucchini, divided into half-moons of 1/2-inch
- 1 tiny red onion, divided into half-moons of 1/4-inch
- 2 mini sweet peppers or 1 bell pepper, sliced into 1/4-inch slices
- 1 (15 oz.) chickpeas, drained Can

- 1/2 teaspoon of cumin
- 1/4 teaspoon coriander
- 1/8 teaspoon cinnamon
- About 1/2 teaspoon salt, and more to taste
- Eggs

Directions:

On a medium-high flame, heat the oil in a skillet over the campfire or camp stove unless hot and glinting.

Put the onions, peppers, and zucchini, and sauté for around 5 minutes before it starts to soften. Mix the drained chickpeas and spices and simmer for about 10 minutes, until the vegetables and chickpeas are cooked and browned in portions.

To make a well in the middle of the plate, transfer the vegetables & chickpeas to the skillet's sides.

If the bottom of the pan is looking dry, apply a little oil. In the well, break two eggs and cook them to your taste. Remove the skillet from the flame and serve.

Nutrition:

Calories 379

Carbohydrates 12g

Proteins 13g

Fat 8g

Banana Coconut French Toast

Preparation Time: 15 minutes

Cooking Time: 6 minutes

Servings: 4

Ingredients:

- 1 lb. loaf of crusty French bread, sliced into 3/4-inch pieces
- 1 quite ripe banana
- 1 (14 oz.) of coconut mil k Can
- 1 teaspoon of cinnamon ground

- 1 teaspoon extract of vanilla
- 1/2 tsp of salt
- Coconut oil

To serve:

- Warmed Maple Syrup Substitute
- Fresh blueberries
- Shredded flakes of coconut

Directions:

Mash the banana until it is soft in a bowl wide enough to fit a slice or two of bread. Mix the coconut milk, cinnamon, vanilla extract, and salt and whisk to blend.

Over medium heat, prepare a nonstick pan. Soak a slice of bread into the batter and let it soak on each side for a couple of seconds.

Let the excess runoff and then fry it on each side, around 3 minutes per side, in the skillet until golden and crispy.

Repeat with the rest of your bread, adding to the pan the coconut oil as required. Enjoy with syrup, fresh blueberries, and shredded coconut. Serve and enjoy.

Nutrition:

Calories 360

Carbohydrates 8g

Proteins 9g

Fat 12g

Turmeric Tofu Scramble

Preparation Time: 15 minutes

Cooking Time: 15 minutes

Servings: 2

Ingredients:

- 2 tablespoons of oil
- Mini potatoes fingerlings
- Mushrooms
- 1 tiny shallot
- 2 cups of spinach

- Tofu around 5 oz, pat dry with a paper towel
- 1/4 teaspoon of turmeric
- 1 tablespoon of nutritional yeast
- 1/4 teaspoon of salt
- 1 pinch of black pepper

Directions:

Cut the potatoes into 1/4" cubes. Cut the mushrooms in the quarter. Slice into half-moons the shallot.

Over medium heat, warm-up 1 tbsp of oil in a pan. When heated, add the potatoes and cook for around 7 minutes, until they start to soften and turn brown.

Add the shallots and mushrooms and cook for 3 minutes, until the mushrooms start to brown and the shallots are tender. Shift to one of the pans' sides.

If required, add another tablespoon of oil. Crumble in the pan the tofu and toss with the oil. Dust the turmeric over the tofu and nutritional yeast, then sauté for 4 minutes.

Transfer the spinach to the pan, then swirl until simmered with the other components of the scramble. Add salt & pepper to taste. Enjoy.

Nutrition:

Calories 270

Carbohydrates 16g

Proteins 14g

Fat 18g

Coconut Chocolate Granola

Preparation Time: 15 minutes

Cooking Time: 20 minutes

Servings: 4

Ingredients:

- 1 cup of oats, rolled
- 1/2 cup of chopped nuts
- 1/4 cup of cacao powder
- 1/4 cup of maple syrup

- 2 tablespoons melted coconut oil
- 1 pinch of salt
- 1 cup of coconut flakes
- 1 tbsp of powdered milk
- 1 oz of Freeze-dried raspberries or other freeze-dried fruit

Directions:

Preheat the oven to 300F. Combine the oats, nuts, cacao powder, maple syrup, molten coconut oil, and salt in a wide bowl until it is covered evenly.

Pour the batter on your baking sheet lined with parchment paper in an even layer. Bake it for 15 minutes.

Remove from the oven the baking sheet, incorporate the coconut, and return for an extra 5 minutes to the oven. Take the granola out of the oven and let it cool thoroughly.

Divide the granola into 4 bags of zip tops. To each bag, add 1 tablespoon powdered milk and 1/4 oz of freeze-dried raspberries.

At the camp, add half a cup of water (hot or cold) to the bag at camp and blend. Enjoy your breakfast.

Nutrition:

Calories 614

Carbohydrate 53g

Proteins 11g

Fat 42g

Poultry

Chicken Meatballs and Pasta

Preparation Time: 10 minutes

Cooking Time: 65 minutes

Servings: 4

Ingredients:

- 3 cups small pasta
- 1 teaspoon olive oil
- 2/3 cup of water
- 1 lb. ground chicken
- 1 egg, lightly beaten
- 1/2 cup of bread crumbs

Salt and pepper

- 2 (12 oz.) jars of marinara sauce, divided
- 3 carrots, sliced into coins
- 1 small zucchini, halved lengthwise and cut into slices
- 1 yellow bell pepper, cored, seeded and cut into strips

Directions:

Preheat your oven.

Place the chicken into a mixing bowl.

Add the egg, breadcrumbs, salt and pepper and mix until well blended.

Shape the mixture into meatballs.

Spray a cooking pan with a non-stick cooking spray, so base, sides and lid are well coated.

Place the pasta into the pan and drizzle with olive oil.

Pour in the water, stirring to coat the pasta well, then pour one jar of marinara sauce over the pasta.

Add layers of carrots, zucchini, and bell pepper strips and pour the second jar of sauce over the vegetables.

Cover and bake 45 minutes or until the vegetables are fork tender.

Nutrition:

Calories: 239 kcal, Protein: 27g, Fat: 14g, Carbs: 0g

One Pot Chicken Rigatoni

Preparation Time: 10 minutes

Cooking Time: 25 minutes

Servings: 4

Ingredients:

- 2 tablespoons extra virgin olive oil
- 1-pound chicken breast, diced
- 2 red peppers, sliced into t hin strips
- 1 (28-ounce) can crushed tomatoes

- 2 cups chicken broth
- 1-pound dry rigatoni
- 2 teaspoons Italian seasoning
- ½ cup Parmesan cheese
- ¼ cup butter
- ¼ cup heavy cream
- Crushed red pepper flakes, optional

Directions:

Place a pot over medium heat (about 20 briquettes) and warm the oil.

Brown the chicken breast.

Add the red pepper strips and sauté for about two minutes, until they begin to soften.

Add the crushed tomatoes, chicken broth, rigatoni, and Italian seasoning.

Cover the pot, and place 6 briquettes on top.

Bring it to a boil and cook for 10–15 minutes, until the pasta is ready.

Remove the pot from the heat and stir in the Parmesan, butter, and cream.

Cover, and let it sit for 5 minutes.

Serve garnished with additional Parmesan and crushed red pepper flakes to taste.

Nutrition:

Calories: 613.5 kcal, Protein: 38.2g, Fat: 7.8g, Carbs: 70.8g

Rice With Chicken & Chorizo

Preparation Time: 10 minutes

Cooking Time: 1 hour and 30 minutes

Servings: 6-8

Ingredients:

- 8 skinless, boneless chicken thighs (or breasts, if you prefer)
- Salt
- Freshly ground black pepper
- 2½ tablespoons extra-virgin olive oil
- 1 onion, chopped
- 3 cloves garlic, minced
- 2 cups long-grain rice
- 2 teaspoons ground cumin
- 2 teaspoons crushed dried oregano leaves

- 5 cups low-sodium chicken broth or stock
- 1 green bell pepper, seeded and diced
- 1¾ cups thick and chunky salsa (mild, medium, or hot)
- ¾ pound spicy chorizo chicken sausage, diced
- 6 to 8 sprigs of cilantro leaves, for garnish
- ¼ cup chopped scallions, for garnish
- 6 to 8 lime wedges, for garnish

Directions:

Preheat the oven to 350°F.

Trim any visible fat from the chicken, and season with salt and pepper.

Set a pot in the medium heated Dutch Oven, add the olive oil. Add half of the chicken pieces, and cook for about 3 minutes. Turn over and cook for 3 minutes, or until the chicken is lightly browned on both sides. Transfer the chicken to a platter, as they cook and repeat with the remaining pieces.

Add more oil to the pot, if needed, and add the onion. Cook until softened. Add the garlic and cook for 2 minutes, or until softened.

Add the rice, cumin, oregano, and some salt, and cook for 2 to 3 minutes, stirring until the rice is coated with oil. Stir in the broth. Add the green pepper and the salsa. Bring to a boil.

Cover, put in the preheated oven, and bake for 30 minutes, or until the liquid is almost completely absorbed.

Stir in the chorizo. Tuck the chicken pieces into the rice mixture, and pour in any juices that have collected on the platter. Cover, return to the oven, and bake for 20 minutes, or until the chicken is cooked through and the rice is tender.

Garnish with the cilantro leaves, chopped scallions, and lime wedges.

Nutrition:

Calories: 480.2 kcal,

Protein: 39g,

Fat: 11.7g,

Carbs: 53.7 g

Chicken and Squash One-Pot Meal

Preparation Time: 10 minutes

Cooking Time: 2 hours

Servings: 4

Ingredients:

- 1 (3–4 pound) fryer/boiler chicken
- 2 teaspoons salt
- 4 cups 1-inch dry bread cubes
- 2 cups butternut squash, cut into ½-inch cubes
- ½ large red onion, chopped
- 4 sprigs fresh thyme

Directions:

Preheat the oven to 375°F (190°C). Place a rack in the lower third.

Pat the chicken dry and season evenly with salt.

Layer the bread cubes and squash over the bottom of the Dutch oven. Add the thyme on top.

Make a well in the center of the Dutch oven and place the chicken in the well. Insert a cooking thermometer in its thigh.

Cover and bake for 1 hour.

Remove the lid and continue to bake for 30 more minutes until the chicken is golden, tender, and crisp. The juices should run clear and the cooking thermometer should read 165°F.

Let cool for a while and then shred the meat.

Serve with the cooked squash and bread mixture.

Nutrition:

Calories: 992 kcal,

Protein: 79g,

Fat: 61g,

Carbs: 27g

Cheesy Baked Chicken Spaghetti Casserole

Preparation Time: 10 minutes

Cooking Time: 65 minutes

Servings: 8

Ingredients:

- 4 bone-in chicken thighs with skin
- 1 teaspoon Italian seasoning
- Salt and pepper to taste
- 1 dash balsamic vinegar
- 1 pound Italian sausages
- ½ pound mushrooms, sliced
- 3 cups spaghetti sauce
- 1 pound spaghetti
- 2 cups shredded Italian cheese blend

Directions:

Preheat the oven to 350°F (175°C).

Boil salted water in a pot and cook the spaghetti partially for 4 minutes. Drain and set aside.

Spray the pot with cooking spray and heat it over medium-high heat.

Add the chicken thighs and stir-cook for 3 minutes per side until evenly browned.

Season with salt, Italian seasoning, and pepper. Transfer to a plate and sprinkle vinegar on top.

Add the sausage and mushrooms to the pot; stir-cook for 4–5 minutes until evenly browned. Drain and remove residual grease.

Add the spaghetti sauce and cooked chicken (skin side up).

Cook for 3–5 minutes until the sauce is bubbly.

Cover and bake for 30 minutes.

Add the spaghetti noodles and Italian cheese blend on top; bake for 10 more minutes until cooked to satisfaction.

Serve warm.

Nutrition: Calories: 614 kcal, Protein: 33g, Fat: 27g, Carbs: 58g

Chicken Stew a la Bonne Femme

Preparation Time: 10 minutes

Cooking Time: 3 hours & 15 minutes

Servings: 4-6

Ingredients:

- 1 pound bacon
- 1 (3-pound) chicken, c ut into pieces
- 3 pounds white potatoes, peeled and cut in chunks
- 2 large onions, peeled and chopped
- 1 large green bell pepper, seeded and chopped
- 2 stalks celery, sliced
- 3 cloves garlic, peeled and minced
- 2 green onions, sliced
- 1/4 cup minced parsley

- 1/2 teaspoon salt
- 1/2 teaspoon freshly cracked black pepper
- 1/4 teaspoon cayenne pepper
- 3 cups chicken broth

Directions:

In an ovenproof pot over medium heat fry bacon until crisp and the fat has rendered, about 8–10 minutes. Remove bacon to a paper towel–lined plate to drain.

Add chicken to bacon drippings remaining in pot and brown well on both sides, about 3 minutes per side. Remove to a plate to rest. Add potato chunks to pot; brown on all sides, about 5 minutes, and remove to rest with the chicken.

In a medium bowl, combine onions, bell pepper, celery, garlic, green onions, and parsley; mix well. In a small bowl combine salt, pepper, and cayenne.

Heat oven to 350°F.

Carefully remove all but 1 or 2 tablespoons of the bacon drippings from pot. Layer the ingredients in Dutch oven in following order: 1/2 each of chicken, potatoes, bacon, vegetable mixture, and seasonings; remaining potatoes, bacon, chicken, vegetable mixture, and seasonings.

Carefully pour broth into the Dutch oven, cover with the lid, and roast for 2 1/2 hours. Let stand 10 minutes before serving.

Nutrition:

Calories: 1097.87 kcal, Protein: 75.56g, Fat: 51.18g, Carbs: 78.9g

Chicken Divan

Preparation Time: 10 minutes

Cooking Time: 55 minutes

Servings: 6

Ingredients:

- 1/4 cup unsalted butter
- 1/4 cup all-purpose flour
- 1 cup chicken broth
- 1 cup milk
- 1/2 teaspoon salt
- 1/2 teaspoon freshly cracked black pepper
- 1/8 teaspoon ground nutmeg

- 1/2 cup freshly grated Parmigiano-Reggiano, divided
- 3 tablespoons dry sherry
- 3 cups cooked chicken, cut into bite-sized pieces
- 1 (1-pound) bag broccoli florets, thawed
- 1 cup slivered almonds, divided
- 1/2 cup heavy cream

Directions:

Heat oven to 350°F.

Melt butter over medium heat in a cooking pan. Add flour and cook, stirring constantly, 1 minute.

Gradually whisk in broth and milk; cook 3 minutes, or until it begins to thicken. Stir in salt, pepper, nutmeg, 1/4 cup cheese, and sherry; cook until cheese melts.

Remove from heat and stir in the chicken, broccoli, half of almonds, and cream. Sprinkle remaining almonds and cheese over the top. Bake uncovered 35 minutes, or until bubbly and golden brown.

Nutrition:

Calories: 242.9 kcal,

Protein: 22.4g,

Fat: 10.1g,

Carbs: 15g

Meat

Apple Cheddar Burgers with Caramelized Onions

Preparation Time: 15 minutes

Cooking Time: 30 minutes

Servings: 6

Ingredients:

For the burgers:

- 1 large apple
- 2 lb. ground beef, 85% lean
- 1 teaspoon salt

For the onions:

- 1 large onion, thinly sliced
- 1/2 teaspoon salt

- 1 tablespoon olive oil

To assemble:

- 6 oz. sharp Vermont cheddar
- 6 hamburger buns
- other condiments of choice

Directions:

Add the olive oil, onions, and salt to a small pan and place at medium to low heat over the fire. Cook, stirring, for about 20-25 minutes, until the onions are soft and begin to caramelize.

In the meantime, peel & grate the apple on a cheese grater's large holes. Mix with the salt and the ground beef, then shape into six patties.

Grill the patties over medium-high heat on each side for around 3-4 minutes. Toast the buns, build the burgers, topping each with the cheddar, caramelized onions, and whatever other condiments you want.

Nutrition:

Calories: 403

Carbs: 38g

Fat: 15g

Protein: 30g

Big Ol' Breakfast Burrito

Preparation Time: 15 minutes

Cooking Time: 60 minutes

Servings: 6

Ingredients:

- 12 eggs
- 1 (1 ounce) packa ge taco seasoning
- 2/3 cup milk
- ½ teaspoon salt
- 2 tablespoon butter
- 2 tablespoon minced garlic
- 1 pound bulk pork sausage
- ½ red onion, diced
- 1 tomato, diced
- ¼ cup chopped fresh cilantro

- 1 (3.5 ounces) can diced jalapenos – optional
- 1 ½ cups shredded Cheddar cheese
- 20 (6 inches) flour tortillas

Directions:

Whisk the eggs, milk, plus salt in your large bowl. Heat-up butter in a large skillet on medium-high heat. Put in the egg batter; cook, then mix within 5 minutes. Chop the cooked eggs, then put them in your large bowl, and set aside.

Heat-up a large skillet on medium heat, then mix in the sausage and garlic. Cook and stir within 5 minutes, then put the onion.

Drain, then remove any excess grease. Mix the sausage, eggs, tomato, cilantro, jalapeno, plus taco seasoning. Let the batter cool at room temperature, then mix in the Cheddar cheese.

Put a tortilla onto your clean work surface, then put some of your filling halfway and the middle of the tortilla.

Flatten your filling into a rectangle shape using the back of a spoon. Fold the bottom of your tortilla over the filling. Fold in the left and right edges.

Roll your burrito up to the top edge, forming a tight cylinder. Repeat with the rest of the fixings.

Wrap each burrito using plastic wrap and freeze until ready to serve. Warm in the microwave until hot, within 3 to 4 minutes, before serving.

Nutrition:

Calories: 590; Carbs: 58g; Fat: 22g; Protein: 31g

Campfire Stuffed Peppers

Preparation Time: 15 minutes

Cooking Time: 30 minutes

Servings: 2-4

Ingredients:

- 2 large green peppers (or 4 small), cut the tops, seeded & devein
- 2 tbsp ketchup
- 1 lb. hamburger
- 1 cup instant rice
- 1/2 tsp salt
- 1/4 tsp black pepper

- 1 tsp dried parsley
- 2 packets of tomato cup of soup
- 1 cup water

Directions:

Preheat the campfire for cooking.

Put the hamburger, rice, salt, pepper, parsley, and ketchup in a medium mixing bowl; mix using your hands until well blended. Stuff it to your peppers equally. Put into a foil pan.

Mix the tomato soup packets plus water, then pour over the stuffed peppers with the pan to catch the rest of the liquid.

Put the pepper tops back on; then wrap with foil and put over the cooking fire's grate for approximately 30 minutes, or until peppers are cooked but not mushy, and the meat is cooked through. Cut into halves with a sharp knife and serve hot.

Nutrition:

Calories: 243

Carbs: 11g

Fat: 15g

Protein: 15g

Classic Beef Kabobs

Preparation Time: 15 minutes

Cooking Time: 9-11 minutes

Servings: 4

Ingredients:

- 2 tablespoons olive oil
- 8 ounces mushrooms
- 1 medium red onion, slice into 1-inch pieces
- 1 pound beef Top Sirloin Steak sliced 1-inch thick
- 1 medium red, yellow/green bell pepper, cut into 1-inch pieces

- Salt
- 2 cloves garlic, minced
- 1/2 teaspoon ground black pepper
- 1 tablespoon chopped fresh oregano or one teaspoon dried oregano leaves

Directions:

Cut the Top Sirloin Boneless steak into bits of 1-inch beef. Combine ingredients to the season in a large bowl. Remove the bits of beef, mushrooms, bell pepper, and onion; mix to coat.

Alternatively, thread beef and vegetable pieces evenly on eight skewers of 12 inches of metal, leaving small spaces between pieces.

Place kabobs on grid over medium coals covered with ash. Grill kabobs, fried, 8-10 minutes (over medium heat on the preheated gas grill, 9-11 minutes) for rare, medium doneness (145 ° F) to medium (160 ° F), turning once. Season salted kabobs, as desired.

Nutrition:

Calories: 140

Carbs: 4g

Fat: 4g

Protein: 22g

Campfire Cajun Sausage and Pepper Foil Packs

Preparation Time: 15 minutes

Cooking Time: 20-25 minutes

Servings: 4

Ingredients:

- 3 garlic cloves, minced
- 2 Tbsp. olive oil
- 1 Tbsp. Cajun seasoning
- 1 green bell pepper, sliced into one-inch strips
- 13 oz. smoked, beef sausage, fully-cooked, sliced into ½-inch slices
- 1 medium white onion, sliced
- Heavy-duty foil
- A red bell pepper, sliced into 1-inch strips
- 1 lb. baby red potatoes, quartered

Directions:

Add a medium-sized bowl of red potatoes, bell peppers, and onion—Toss vegetable mixture in the seasoning with olive oil, garlic, and Cajun.

Place a heavy-duty aluminum foil sheet 18 "x12 "onto a flat surface. Apply 1/4 of the vegetable mixture to the foil center.

Top the vegetables with 1/4 of the sliced sausage (about 1 component in each). Fold in the right and left sides, then roll to come together.

Fold in and turn the top and bottom edges to seal the envelope. Repeat for a total of 4 packets with the remaining mixture. (Wrap foil packets with a second layer of foil to prevent bursting when cooking on a campfire)

Build and start a fire within a fire ring or other structure made of metal. Place a grate over the flames, straight above the gas. Place foil packs with pliers on the hot grate.

Cook for 20-25 minutes, flipping through halfway until potatoes are fork-tender and sausage is heated.

Nutrition:

Calories: 349

Carbs: 44g

Fat: 10g

Protein: 21g

Texas BBQ Bloody Mary

Preparation Time: 15 minutes

Cooking Time: 0 minutes

Servings: 1

Ingredients:

- 2 oz. vodka
- 1 Tbsp. smoky Texas BBQ sauce
- Celery salt to taste
- 4 oz. tomato juice
- 1 tsp. Worcestershire sauce
- ½ tsp. hot sauce
- ½ lemon, juiced
- Optional garnishes:
- Brisket slice
- Smoked salt
- Cherry tomatoes
- Celery stalk

- Olives
- Lemon wedges
- Grilled jalapeño

Directions:

Add all ingredients into ice-filled cocktail shaker and shake for 10 seconds. Serve drinks and garnish over sugar.

Nutrition:

Calories: 280

Carbs: 35g

Fat: 0g

Protein: 0g

Lights Frito Pie

Preparation Time: 15 minutes

Cooking Time: 1 hour & 10 minutes

Servings: 5

Ingredients:

- 2 lbs. Ground Beef
- 1 onion, diced
- 1 tsp. olive oil
- 1 clove garlic, minced
- ¼ tsp. cayenne
- 1 tsp. ground cumin
- 2 Tbsp. chili powder
- Salt
- 1 ½ cups of beer

- 2 Tbsp. cornmeal or masa harina
- 8 bags (1-2 oz) of corn chips
- 1 can of diced tomatoes & green chilis
- 1 can (8 oz.) of tomato sauce
- 1 ½ cups grated cheddar cheese

Directions:

Heat a large non-stick pan until hot over medium heat. Add ground beef and cook for 8-10 minutes, stirring occasionally and breaking the beef into small crumbles. Cut the beef off and set it aside to drain.

To the skillet, add olive oil and onion; cook until well browned. In addition to garlic, chili powder, cayenne, cumin, and salt, add ground beef back in. Stir to blend.

Attach the bottle, the diced tomatoes, the green chilis, and the tomato sauce and bring to a low level. Cover with a lid and allow bubbling and cooking to reduce and thicken the sauce and enhance the flavors for about 1 hour.

Stir in the cornmeal after an hour, which will help to thicken the sauce. When the sauce gets too thick, add a little water and if it is not thick enough, keep cooking until the desired consistency is achieved.

Slice or flip the bags open, and spoon the chili over the corn chips. Then a sprinkle of cheddar cheese over each bag. Enable to melt slightly and then serve and enjoy.

Nutrition:

Calories: 287; Carbs: 8g; Fat: 21g; Protein: 16g

Seafood

Lime-Drizzled Fish Tacos

Preparation Time: 15 minutes

Cooking Time: 10 minutes

Servings: 4

Ingredients:

- 4 Tilapia fish filets
- ¼ cup chipotle dressing
- 1 cup cilantro, chopped

- 2 tomatoes, diced
- 1 red onion, diced
- 2 limes, juiced
- 8 tacos Vegetable oil Marinade
- 3 tablespoons honey
- 1 teaspoon cumin
- 1 teaspoon oregano
- 1 teaspoon cayenne pepper
- 1 lime, juiced
- ¼ cup extra virgin olive oil

Directions:

Combine the ingredients for the marinade. Place the tilapia in a dish with the marinade and allow the fish to marinate for an hour.

Bring the fire to medium-high, coat a little vegetable oil on the grid. Ensure that the tilapia is about 5 inches from the flames, grill until the fish is flakey for 8 minutes.

Heat the tacos for a minute on the grill. Cover with cilantro tacos, tomatoes, red onions, and chipotle sauce, flake tuna, drizzle with lime juice and break between tacos.

Nutrition:

Calories: 246

Carbs: 25g

Fat: 3g

Protein: 24g

Orange Bacon Salmon Skewers

Preparation Time: 15 minutes

Cooking Time: 10 minutes

Servings: 4

Ingredients:

- 1 pound salmon filets
- 2 oranges, segmented
- 8 bacon slices

Directions:

Sliced salmon into 1-inch bits. Place the salmon on the skewers with orange segments. Wrap per skewer with 2 slices of bacon.

Cook the salmon over the fire while holding it 6 inches over the fire and 6 inches above the fire—Cook for 7 minutes or so.

Nutrition:

Calories: 183

Carbs: 4g

Fat: 10g

Protein: 19g

Grilled Shrimp and Mushrooms

Preparation Time: 15 minutes

Cooking Time: 6 minutes

Servings: 4

Ingredients:

- 1½ pounds jumbo shrimp, shelled and deveined
- 12 Cremini mushrooms 8 garlic cloves, finely chopped
- 1 lemon, juiced
- ½ teaspoon paprika

- ½ teaspoon salt
- ½ teaspoon black pepper
- ¼ teaspoon extra virgin olive oil
- Vegetable oil

Directions:

Combine the cinnamon, black pepper, paprika, lemon juice, and garlic with extra virgin olive oil. Marinate the shrimp and mushrooms for an hour with the marinade.

Thread mushrooms and shrimp on skewers. Use a little vegetable oil to spray your grill and fire to medium.

Cook the mushroom shrimp skewers for about 6 minutes and serve them with a salad.

Nutrition:

Calories: 90

Carbs: 0g

Fat: 1g

Protein: 22g

Ying and Yang Salmon

Preparation Time: 15 minutes

Cooking Time: 10 minutes

Servings: 4

Ingredients:

- 4 6-ounce wild salmon steaks
- 2 teaspoon Mirin
- 1 lemon, juiced
- 4 tablespoons soy sauce
- ¼ cup honey
- Vegetable Oil

Directions:

Combine the mirin, lemon juice, honey, and soy sauce. Put the marinade on the salmon steaks. Enable it for an hour to marinate.

Heat-up your grill to high, and grease the grates loosely. Brush the honey with the salmon and put it on the grill.

Cook for 10 minutes, turning over as the fish releases itself from the grater happily. After 5 minutes, this could occur. Serve the fish with grilled vegetables and rice.

Nutrition:

Calories: 210

Carbs: 28g

Fat: 4g

Protein: 17g

Tequila Jalapeño Scallops

Preparation Time: 15 minutes

Cooking Time: 4 minutes

Servings: 4

Ingredients:

- 1½ pounds scallops
- ¼ cup tequila
- 1 lime, juiced
- 2 jalapeños, sliced
- 1 teaspoon salt
- 1 teaspoon black pepper
- Vegetable oil

Directions:

Combine the tequila, lime juice, salt, black pepper, and jalapeños and marinate for 15 minutes with the scallops. Per skewer, position 3 scallops.

Heat a medium-high grill and spray with vegetable oil. Place skewers so that the scallops are flat out on the grill. For 2 minutes, grill each side. Serve with noodles and a tequila shot!

Nutrition:

Calories: 50; Carbs: 4g; Fat: 0g; Protein: 9g

Grilled Snapper

Preparation Time: 15 minutes

Cooking Time: 8 minutes

Servings: 4

Ingredients:

- 4 red snapper fish
- 1 lemon, sliced
- 1-2 lemons, juiced
- Salt and pepper
- Extra virgin olive oil

Directions:

For roasting, grab 4 sticks or skewers. Place a skewer through the fish, brush the fish with a little extra virgin olive oil, sprinkle with salt and pepper, and stick a lemon slice on each side of the fish.

Hold the fish about 6 inches above the flames, and cook for about 8 minutes. Drizzle with salt and lemon juice, if needed. Enjoy! Enjoy!

Nutrition:

Calories: 101

Carbs: 0g

Fat: 1g

Protein: 21g

Swordfish Steak Skewers

Preparation Time: 15 minutes

Cooking Time: 0 minutes

Servings: 4

Ingredients:

- 1 pound swordfish steak
- 1 red onion, quartered
- 2 red bell peppers, seeded
- ½ teaspoon cayenne pepper
- 1 teaspoon salt
- 1 teaspoon black pepper
- 6 tablespoons extra virgin olive oil

Directions:

Split the swordfish into 1-inch pieces. Cut into 1-inch bits of red bell pepper. Thread the swordfish, bell pepper, and the skewer with the red onion.

Place the cayenne, cinnamon, black pepper, and 6 tablespoons of extra virgin olive oil together. Dust the swordfish and the marinade vegetables.

Steam a medium fire and spray the grid with gasoline. Place skewers of fish on the rack and grill for about 8 minutes or until the fish is flaky. Serve with a healthy green salad.

Nutrition:

Calories: 140; Carbs: 0g; Fat: 5g; Protein: 22g

Vegetables

Tofu Skewers with Spicy Peanut Sauce

Preparation Time: 1 hour

Cooking Time: 15 minutes

Servings: 8

Ingredients:

For the grilled tofu skewers:

- 1 package extra-firm tofu, drained and pressed for 30 minutes or longer
- 2 tablespoons soy sauce
- 2 tablespoons water
- 1 tablespoon honey
- 1/2 teaspoon smoked paprika
- 1/2 teaspoon garlic powder

For the spicy peanut sauce:

- 1/2 cup creamy peanut butter
- 1/4 cup coconut milk
- 2 tablespoons soy sauce
- 2 tablespoons lime juice
- 1 tablespoon Sriracha
- 1/4 teaspoon garlic powder

Directions:

Cut the pressed block of tofu into 8 sticks.

Add the tofu, soy sauce, water, honey, smoked paprika, and garlic powder to a sealable plastic bag, seal, and toss to coat.

Refrigerate for a minimum of 1 hour or 24 hours before grilling.

Mix together all of the spicy peanut sauce ingredients in a small mixing bowl; set aside or refrigerate until needed.

Before grilling, pour the marinade into a bowl to use as a baste.

Thread the tofu onto metal skewers lengthwise.

Preheat the griddle to medium-high heat.

Grill the skewers for 10 to 15 minutes, turning as needed until char marks form on each side; baste with the leftover marinade often as they cook.

Serve hot with the spicy peanut sauce on the side for dipping.

Nutrition:

Calories: 138,

Sodium: 315 mg,

Dietary Fiber: 1.3g,

Fat: 10.6.g,

Carbohydrates: 7.8g

Protein: 5.7g

Marinated Mushroom Kabobs

Preparation Time: 10 minutes

Cooking Time: 10 minutes

Servings: 4

Ingredients:

- 1 punnet white button mushrooms, whole
- 1 green pepper, deseeded and cut into 2-inch pieces
- 1 yellow pepper, deseeded and cut into 2-inch pieces
- 1 onion, cut into 2-inch pieces
- 1-pint cherry tomatoes

For the marinade:

- 1/4 cup olive oil
- 2 cloves garlic, minced
- 1 lemon, juiced
- 1/2 teaspoon dried oregano
- 1/2 teaspoon sea salt

Directions:

Arrange vegetables on metal skewers in an alternating pattern. Place on a baking sheet or piece of aluminum foil. Whisk together the marinade ingredients in a small mixing bowl and pour over skewers; turn skewers to coat well. Preheat a grill to medium heat and cook 4 to 5 minutes on both sides until charred. Remove kabobs to a serving tray and enjoy!

Nutrition:

Calories: 173,

Sodium: 243 mg,

Dietary Fiber: 4.2g,

Fat: 13.2.g,

Carbohydrates: 16.1g

Protein: 2.7g

Creamy Grilled Potato Salad

Preparation Time: 35 minutes

Cooking Time: 10 minutes

Servings: 8

Ingredients:

- 2 (1.5 lb.) bags baby white potatoes
- Non-stick cooking spray

For the dressing:

- ½ cup mayonnaise
- 1 tablespoon sour cream
- 2 teaspoons apple cider vinegar
- 1 tablespoon fresh parsley, chopped
- 1 tablespoon fresh basil, chopped
- 1 teaspoon celery seed
- 1 tablespoon Dijon mustard
- 1 tablespoon lemon juice
- 2 tablespoons olive oil
- ½ teaspoon sea salt
- ½ teaspoon black pepper

Directions:

Preheat grill to medium-high, and spray with non-stick cooking spray.

Place potatoes on griddle and cook until tender, about 10 minutes.

Remove potatoes from grill and allow to cool for 10 minutes.

Combine dressing ingredients in a large mixing bowl and whisk until well-combined.

Fold in the potatoes until mixed well, and serve at room temperature or well-chilled from the refrigerator overnight.

Nutrition:

Calories: 132,

Sodium: 246 mg,

Dietary Fiber: 1.3g,

Fat: 8.9.g,

Carbohydrates: 13.7g,

Protein: 1.9g

Balsamic Glazed Veggie Kabobs

Preparation Time: 10 minutes

Cooking Time: 8 minutes

Servings: 4 to 6

Ingredients:

- ½ cup eggplant, cubed into 1-inch chunks
- ½ cup bell peppers, cubed into 1-inch chunks
- ½ cup zucchini, cubed into 1-inch chunks
- ½ cup red onion, cubed into 1-inch chunks
- 3 tablespoons olive oil
- 1 teaspoon garlic powder
- 1 teaspoon sea salt
- 1 teaspoon black pepper
- 1/4 cup balsamic glaze

Directions:

Preheat griddle to medium-high heat.

Arrange vegetables on metal skewers in an alternating pattern.

Place on a baking sheet or piece of aluminum foil.

Whisk together the olive oil, garlic powder, salt, and pepper in a small mixing bowl and pour over skewers; turn skewers to coat well.

Preheat a grill to medium heat.

Brush skewers with balsamic glaze and cook 4 to 5 minutes on both sides until charred; basting with extra glaze often until vegetables are tender.

Remove kabobs to a serving tray and enjoy!

Nutrition:

Calories: 73,

Sodium: 314 mg,

Dietary Fiber: 0.9g,

Fat: 7.1.g,

Carbohydrates: 3.1g,

Protein: 0.5g

Potato Salad with Bacon Vinaigrette

Preparation Time: 20 minutes

Cooking Time: 40 minutes

Servings: 4

Ingredients:

For the potatoes:

- 7 medium red potatoes, quartered
- 1 sweet potato, peeled and cut into large chunks
- 1/4 cup mayonnaise
- 1 tablespoon Dijon mustard
- 2 teaspoons onion powder
- 2 teaspoons garlic powder
- 1/4 teaspoon celery seed
- Sea salt, to taste
- Freshly ground black pepper, to taste
- For the vinaigrette:
- 2 slices bacon, cooked and chopped
- 1/4 cup extra-virgin olive oil
- 2 tablespoons red wine vinegar
- 2 shallots, minced
- 2 tablespoons fresh parsley, chopped

Directions:

Preheat a griddle to medium.

Put the red potatoes in a large saucepan and cover with cold water by 2 inches. Bring the water to a boil over high heat; after about 10 minutes, add the sweet potatoes.

Return to a boil and cook 10 additional minutes.

Drain the potatoes and set aside to cool.

Whisk the mayonnaise, mustard, onion powder, garlic powder, celery seed, salt and black pepper in medium mixing bowl.

Fold the cooled potatoes into the mayonnaise mixture.

Mix the vinaigrette ingredients together in a small bowl until well-combined.

Use tongs to place the potato pieces back on the hot grill and cook on all sides long enough to cook through and make grill marks, about 1 to 2 minutes per side: be sure to handle the potatoes gently so they don't fall apart.

Remove the potatoes from the grill and place in the bowl with the vinaigrette.

Gently toss to coat completely and serve warm or cold.

Nutrition:

Calories: 521,

Fat: 22.3.g,

Carbohydrates: 72.1g,

Protein: 12g

Artichokes with Harissa-Honey Dip

Preparation Time: 10 minutes

Cooking Time: 30 minutes

Servings: 4

Ingredients:

- 4 medium artichokes
- 1 lemon, juiced
- 4 tablespoons olive oil
- For the Harissa Dip:
- 1/2 cup mayonnaise
- 1 tablespoon harissa
- 1 tablespoon honey
- 1/4 teaspoon fresh ground pepper
- ¼ teaspoon sea salt

Directions:

Cut a 1/2 inch off the top of each artichoke, then cut each in half vertically.

Trim the pointy ends off the leaves with scissors.

Cut out the fuzzy choke in the center of each and discard.

Fill a large pot with water and fit with a steaming rack. Place artichokes on rack and steam until they are tender and easily pierced with a fork, about 30 minutes.

Set aside to cool for 15 minutes.

Preheat grill to high heat.

Combine Harissa Dip ingredients in a small mixing bowl until well-combined and set aside.

Add lemon and oil to a large mixing bowl, and toss artichokes in lemon and oil.

Grill artichokes, cut side down, until nicely charred, about 4 to 5 minutes.

Serve hot with harissa dip.

Nutrition

Calories: 328,

Sodium: 492 mg,

Dietary Fiber: 7.4g,

Fat: 24.7.g,

Carbohydrates: 27.7g,

Protein: 4.9g

Cumin Chili Potato Wedges

Preparation Time: 5 minutes

Cooking Time: 20 minutes

Servings: 3 to 4

Ingredients:

- 3 large russet potatoes, scrubbed and cut into 1-inch thick wedges
- 1/3 cup olive oil
- 1 teaspoon cumin
- 1 teaspoon chili powder
- 1 teaspoon garlic powder
- 1 teaspoon kosher salt
- 1 teaspoon freshly ground black pepper

Directions:

Mix together the cumin, chili powder, garlic powder, salt, and pepper in a small bowl and set aside. Preheat one side of the grill to medium-high heat and the other on medium heat. Brush the potatoes all over with olive oil and place over the hot side of the grill and cook until browned and crisp on both sides, about 2 to 3 minutes per side. Move the potatoes to the cooler side of the grill, tent with foil, and continue to grill until cooked through, about 5 to 10 minutes longer. Remove the potatoes from the grill to a large bowl. Sprinkle with the spice mixture and toss to coat. Serve warm and enjoy.

Nutrition:

Calories: 343,

Sodium: 606 mg,

Dietary Fiber: 7.1g,

Fat: 17.3.g,

Carbohydrates: 44.9g,

Protein: 5g

Soups

Thai Curry Pumpkin Soup

Preparation Time: 5 minutes

Cooking Time: 15 minutes

Servings: 6

Ingredients:

- 3 tablespoons cooking oil
- 1-3 tbsp Thai red curry paste
- 6 cups vegetable broth
- 3 (15-ounce) cans pumpkin puree
- 1½ (14-ounce) cans coconut milk
- kosher salt
- ¼ cup chopped cilantro

Directions:

Set the Dutch oven over a bed of 15 hot coals. Add the oil, and when it begins to simmer, add the curry paste. Cook, stirring, for 1 minute.

Add the broth and pumpkin puree, stirring to mix well, and bring to a boil. Mix in the coconut milk and boil again.

Cook within 10 minutes, stirring frequently and reducing the heat as needed by removing coals from beneath the pot. Taste and add salt as needed. Stir in the cilantro and serve hot.

Nutrition:

Calories: 105; Carbs: 9g; Fat: 6g; Protein: 2g

Italian Tomato and Orzo Soup

Preparation Time: 5 minutes

Cooking Time: 25 minutes

Servings: 6

Ingredients:

- 2 tablespoons olive oil
- 1 onion, diced
- 8 cups vegetable broth
- 2 (14-ounce) cans Italian-style diced tomatoes (with garlic and herbs), with their juice
- 1 teaspoon kosher salt
- ½ teaspoon freshly ground black pepper
- 2 cups (about 12 ounces) orzo pasta or other small pasta
- 4 cups (loosely packed) spinach

Directions:

Set the Dutch oven over a bed of 15 hot coals. Add the oil, and when it begins to simmer, add the onion. Cook, occasionally stirring, until soft, about 5 minutes.

Add the broth, tomatoes and their juice, salt, and pepper. Bring to a boil and cook, occasionally stirring, for 10 to 15 minutes.

Put the pasta, then cook, occasionally stirring, until tender, about 5 to 6 minutes (check the package's directions). Mix in the spinach, then cook until wilted, within 2 more minutes. Serve hot.

Nutrition:

Calories: 322

Carbs: 29g

Fat: 11g

Protein: 26g

Bread Soup with Greens

Preparation Time: 5 minutes

Cooking Time: 35 minutes

Servings: 4-6

Ingredients:

- 2 tablespoons olive oil
- 1 onion, diced
- 10 to 12 leaves hearty greens (kale, chard, mustard, etc.), tough center ribs removed, leaves julienned
- 1 teaspoon kosher salt
- ½ teaspoon freshly ground black pepper
- 1 (14-ounce) can cannellini beans
- 4 cups vegetable broth
- 2 cups stale French bread, crusts removed, torn or cut into ½-inch pieces

Directions:

Set the Dutch oven over a bed of 12 hot coals and heat the olive oil. Add the onion and cook, frequently stirring, until soft, about 5 minutes.

Add the greens, salt, and pepper and cook, stirring, until the greens begin to wilt. If needed to prevent burning, add about ¼ cup of water.

Put the beans plus broth, and bring to a simmer. Stir in the bread. Cover the pot and remove 2 or 3 of the coals from underneath.

Simmer, occasionally stirring, for about 30 minutes, until the bread dissolves into the soup and thickens it. Serve hot.

Nutrition:

Calories: 133

Carbs: 23g

Fat: 2g

Protein: 0g

Butternut Squash and White Bean Stew

Preparation Time: 5 minutes

Cooking Time: 40 minutes

Servings: 8

Ingredients:

- 2 tablespoons olive oil
- 1 onion, diced
- 2 garlic cloves, minced
- 4 cups cubed, peeled butternut squash
- 1 (14-ounce) can diced tomatoes
- 1 teaspoon kosher salt
- ½ teaspoon freshly ground black pepper
- 2 cups of water
- 2 (15-ounce) cans cannellini beans, drained & rinsed

Directions:

Heat-up the oil in the Dutch oven set over a bed of 12 hot coals. Add the onion and cook, frequently stirring, until soft, about 5 minutes.

Stir in the garlic, squash, tomatoes, salt, and pepper. Add the water and bring to a simmer. Remove 2 or 3 of the coals underneath the pot, cover, and let simmer for about 25 minutes, until the squash is tender.

Mix in the beans, then continues to simmer, uncovered, occasionally stirring, until the beans are heated through, and the liquid has cooked down a bit, about 10 minutes. Serve hot.

Nutrition:

Calories: 214

Carbs: 39g

Fat: 3g

Protein: 11g

Green Chile And Corn Chowder

Preparation Time: 5 minutes

Cooking Time: 20 minutes

Servings: 4

Ingredients:

- 1 tablespoon olive oil
- 1 onion, chopped
- 1 (16-ounce) package frozen corn, thawed
- 2 cups whole milk, divided
- 1 (14-ounce) can fire-roasted diced green chilis
- ¾ teaspoon kosher salt
- 1 cup sharp cheddar cheese, shredded, divided

Directions:

Heat-up the oil in the Dutch oven set over a bed of 10 hot coals. Add the onion and cook, occasionally stirring, until soft, about 5 minutes.

Add the corn and continue to cook for about 3 minutes, until the corn begins to soften. Add the milk, chilis, and salt and bring to a simmer.

Cook, frequently stirring, removing coals from underneath the pot if necessary to keep the soup from boiling, until heated through and the corn is very tender about 10 more minutes

Stir in half of the cheese until it is melted and incorporated. Serve hot, garnished with the remaining cheese.

Nutrition:

Calories: 187

Carbs: 25g

Fat: 7g

Protein: 0g

Fish Stew with Tomatoes

Preparation Time: 5 minutes

Cooking Time: 20 minutes

Servings: 4-6

Ingredients:

- 6 tablespoons olive oil
- 1 onion, diced
- 1 (14-ounce) can Italian-style diced tomatoes (with garlic and herbs), with their juice
- 1 cup dry white wine (or substitute broth or water)
- 1 cup of water
- 1 teaspoon kosher salt
- ½ teaspoon freshly ground black pepper
- 1½ pounds frozen fish fillets (any mild white fish, such as cod, halibut, sea bass, or red snapper)

Directions:

Heat the olive oil in the Dutch oven set over a bed of 10 hot coals. Put the onion, then cook, stirring, until soft, within 5 minutes.

Put the tomatoes, plus their juice, and simmer for about 10 more minutes. Add the wine (or broth or water), water, salt, pepper, and fish, and bring to a simmer. Cook, occasionally stirring, until the fish is cooked through, about 5 to 7 minutes. Serve hot.

Nutrition:

Calories: 190; Carbs: 5g; Fat: 1g; Protein: 9g

Spiced Chickpea and Potato Stew

Preparation Time: 5 minutes

Cooking Time: 25 minutes

Servings: 6

Ingredients:

- 2 tablespoons cooking oil
- 3 shallots, diced
- 1 tablespoon grated fresh ginger
- 2 cups diced potatoes
- 2 tablespoons curry powder
- 1 teaspoon kosher salt
- ½ teaspoon freshly ground black pepper
- 2 cans chickpeas, drained & rinsed well
- 3 cups of water

Directions:

Heat-up the oil in the Dutch oven set over a bed of 10 hot coals. Add the shallots and cook, stirring, until soft, about 5 minutes. Stir in the ginger and cook for about 1 more minute.

Stir in the potatoes, curry powder, salt, and pepper and cook, stirring, for 2 minutes. Add the chickpeas and water. Bring to a simmer.

Remove 2 of the coals from underneath the pot and let simmer, uncovered, for about 15 minutes, until the potatoes are tender and the sauce is thick. Serve hot.

Nutrition:

Calories: 315

Carbs: 50g

Fat: 10g

Protein: 8g

Desserts

Brown Sugar Berry Crisp

Preparation Time: 5 minutes

Cooking Time: 30 minutes

Servings: 6

Ingredients:

- Cooking oil to prepare the Dutch oven
- 6 cups fresh berries (blueberries, blackberries, strawberries, raspberries, or a combination)
- ½ cup plus ⅓ cup light brown sugar, divided
- 2 tablespoons water
- 2 tablespoons cornstarch
- ½ cup uncooked oats
- ¼ cup all-purpose flour
- ½ cup (1 stick) unsalted butter, melted

Directions:

Lightly oil the Dutch oven. In the Dutch oven, toss together the berries, ⅓ cup of the brown sugar, water, and cornstarch. In a small bowl, stir together the oats, flour, the remaining ½ cup of brown sugar, and butter. Sprinkle the oat mixture evenly over the berries. Cover the Dutch oven with the lid. Set the Dutch oven over a bed of 7 hot coals, cover, and place 21 hot coals on the lid. Bake for 25 to 30 minutes, until the fruit is bubbling and the topping is golden brown. Serve warm.

Nutrition:

Calories 216.2,

Total Fat 4.2 g,

Cholesterol 5.1 mg,

Sodium 15.5 mg,

Potassium 162.7 mg,

Total Carbohydrate 40.1 g,

Dietary Fiber 6.1 g,

Sugars 4.9 g,

Protein   6.2 g

Gooey Caramel Baked Apples

Preparation Time: 10 minutes

Cooking Time: 45 minutes

Servings: 8

Ingredients:

- 4 large, crisp apples
- 4 caramels
- 3 tablespoons unsalted butter, melted
- ¼ cup (packed) brown sugar
- 1½ tablespoons all-purpose flour
- 1½ teaspoons cinnamon

Directions:

Cut the apples in half and scoop out the core from each half using a small metal spoon. Cut 2 concentric circles into the apple halves around the scooped-out centers. Turn the apples over and make several slits without cutting through the center of the apple. Arrange the apple halves in the Dutch oven, cut side up. Place a caramel into the center of each apple half. In a small bowl, stir together the butter, brown sugar, flour, and cinnamon. Spoon this mixture over the apple halves in the Dutch oven, dividing evenly. Place the lid on the Dutch oven. Place the Dutch oven over a bed of 6 hot coals and place 20 hot coals on the lid. Bake for 35 to 45 minutes, until the apples are tender. Serve warm.

Nutrition:

Calories 224.4,

Total Fat 6.4 g,

Cholesterol 0.1 mg,

Sodium 404.3 mg,

Potassium 175.4 mg,

Total Carbohydrate 47.2 g,

Dietary Fiber 3.5 g,

Sugars 0.2 g,

Protein   1.8 g

Nutty Salted Caramel Popcorn

Preparation Time: 5 minutes

Cooking Time: 5 minutes

Servings: 6

Ingredients:

- 1 cup (2 sticks) unsalted butter
- 1¼ cups brown sugar
- ½ cup corn syrup
- ½ teaspoon kosher salt
- 6 cups popped popcorn
- ½ cup chopped salted peanuts

Directions:

Place the Dutch oven over a bed of 15 hot coals. Add the butter, brown sugar, corn syrup, and salt, and cook. Stir until the butter melts and the mixture thickens and darkens a bit.

Remove the Dutch oven from the heat and stir in the popcorn and peanuts until well coated. Transfer the mixture in heaping spoonful to wax paper and let cool before serving.

Nutrition:

Calories 381,

Total Fat 1.4 g,

Cholesterol 0 mg,

Sodium 286 mg,

Potassium 110 mg,

Total Carbohydrate 90 g,

Dietary fiber 2.5 g,

Sugar 65 g,

Protein 2 g

Quick And Easy Peach Pie

Preparation Time: 10 minutes, plus 1 hour for pie to cool

Cooking Time: 40 minutes

Servings: 8

Ingredients:

- 1 (9-inch) prepared piecrust
- ¾ cup sugar
- 2 tablespoons unsalted butter, at room temperature
- ⅓ cup all-purpose flour
- ¼ teaspoon ground nutmeg
- 6 peaches, peeled, pitted, and sliced

Directions:

If using a flat piecrust, press it into the bottom and up the sides of an aluminum pie tin (be sure the pie tin will fit in the Dutch oven). Crimp the edges, cutting off any excess.

In a medium bowl, stir together the sugar and butter to mix well. Stir in the flour and nutmeg, and mix until it resembles a coarse meal. Spread half of this flour mixture over the bottom of the piecrust. Arrange the peach slices over the top of the butter-flour mixture, overlapping them as needed, and then sprinkle the remaining butter-flour mixture over the top. Place the pie in the Dutch oven and cover with the lid.

Set the Dutch oven on a bed of 6 hot coals and place 20 hot coals on the lid. Bake for about 40 minutes, until the crust is browned and the filling is bubbling. Remove the Dutch oven from the heat and let the pie cool for at least an hour before serving.

Camp Hack:

You can make your own piecrust, but the simplest way to make this is to buy a prepared refrigerated piecrust in an aluminum foil tin. Alternatively, you can make a crust from scratch at home, press it into a disposable aluminum pie tin, freeze it, and then stash it in your cooler.

Nutrition:

Calories 191.1,

Total Fat 6.2 g,

Sodium   185.5 mg,

Potassium 188.8 mg,

Total Carbohydrate 32.9 g,

Dietary Fiber 2.2 g,

Sugars 14.4 g,

Protein   2.7 g

Pineapple Upside-Down Cake

Preparation Time: 10 minutes

Cooking Time: 25 minutes

Servings: 8

Ingredients:

- 1 cup (2 sticks) unsalted butter, at room temperature, divided
- ¾ cup white sugar
- 2 large eggs, beaten
- 2 cups self-rising flour
- 1 can sliced pineapple rings in juice, drained, ½ cup of the juice reserved
- ¼ cup brown sugar

Directions:

In a large bowl, combine ¾ cup (1½ sticks) of the butter with the sugar and stir until well combined and creamy. Add the eggs and mix until incorporated. Add the flour and stir to combine. Stir in the reserved pineapple juice.

Place the Dutch oven over a bed of 8 hot coals. Add the remaining ¼ cup of butter and the brown sugar to the pot and cook, stirring frequently, until the mixture bubbles and darkens a bit, about 3 minutes.

Remove the pot from the heat and spread the butter and brown sugar mixture out evenly over the bottom of the Dutch oven and arrange the pineapple rings in a single layer on top. Pour the cake batter over the pineapple and place the lid on the pot. Return the pot to the heat.

Place 15 hot coals on the lid of the Dutch oven. Bake for about 20 minutes and then check for doneness (a wooden skewer or toothpick inserted into the center will come out clean). Continue to cook, if necessary, checking every few minutes until done.

Remove the pot from the heat and let cool for about 5 minutes. Place a large plate on top of the pot and invert the pot (carefully, with heatproof gloves protecting your hands and forearms) so that the cake releases onto the plate. Serve warm or at room temperature.

Camp Hack:

To make it easier to get the cake out of the pot—and to make cleanup easier—line the Dutch oven with heavy-duty aluminum foil before adding the butter and brown sugar.

Nutrition:

Calories 319,

Total Fat 12 g,

Cholesterol 22 mg,

Sodium 319 mg,

Potassium 112 mg,

Total Carbohydrate 51 g,

Dietary fiber 0.8 g,

Protein 3.5 g

Buttermilk Chocolate Cake

Preparation Time: 10 minutes

Cooking Time: 50 minutes

Servings: 8

Ingredients:

- 1 cup cooking oil, plus additional for preparing the Dutch oven
- 1 cup buttermilk
- 2 large eggs, beaten
- 2 cups self-rising flour
- 2 cups sugar
- ¾ cup unsweetened cocoa powder
- 1 cup boiling water

Directions:

Lightly oil the Dutch oven with cooking oil.

In a large bowl, whisk together the oil, buttermilk, and eggs.

In a separate bowl, combine the flour, sugar, and cocoa. Mix to combine well.

Add the dry ingredients gradually to the wet ingredients, whisking until the batter is smooth. Stir in the boiling water.

Transfer the batter to the Dutch oven and cover with the lid.

Place the Dutch oven on a bed of 8 hot coals and place 16 hot coals on the lid. Bake for 45 to 50 minutes, until a wooden skewer or toothpick inserted into the center of the cake comes out clean.

Variation: If you don't have buttermilk, you can substitute sour cream or plain yogurt thinned with a little milk, or regular milk "acidified" by adding a tablespoon of vinegar or lemon juice to a cup of regular milk.

Nutrition:

Calories 279.3,

Total Fat 10.4 g,

Cholesterol 56.8 mg,

Sodium 286.2 mg,

Potassium 115.9 mg,

Total Carbohydrate 41.9 g,

Dietary Fiber 1.0 g,

Sugars 17.5 g,

Protein   5.2 g

Double-Chocolate Brownies

Preparation Time: 5 minutes

Cooking Time: 30 minutes

Servings: 8 to 10

Ingredients:

- ¾ cup (1½ sticks) unsalted butter, melted, plus additional for preparing the Dutch oven
- ¾ cup all-purpose flour
- 1½ cups sugar
- ½ cup cocoa powder
- ¼ teaspoon kosher salt
- 3 large eggs, beaten
- 1 cup semisweet chocolate chips

Directions:

Lightly coat the Dutch oven with butter.

In a medium bowl, mix together the flour, sugar, cocoa powder, and salt. In a small bowl, whisk the melted butter and eggs together. Add the egg mixture to the dry ingredients and stir to combine. Stir in the chocolate chips. Pour the batter into the prepared Dutch oven and cover with the lid.

Place the Dutch oven on a bed of 10 hot coals and place 18 hot coals on the lid. Bake for 20 minutes and then check to see if the brownies are done (a wooden skewer or toothpick inserted into the center will come out clean). If necessary, continue cooking, checking every 3 to 5 minutes, until done. Remove the Dutch oven from the heat and let the brownies cool for 10 to 15 minutes before cutting into squares and serving.

Variation: Add a cup of chopped walnuts along with the chocolate chips, if desired.

Nutrition:

Calories 107.4,

Total Fat1.6 g,

Cholesterol 0.0 mg,

Sodium 136.9 mg,

Potassium 75.6 mg,

Total Carbohydrate 23.6 g,

Dietary Fiber 1.5 g,

Sugars 19.3 g,

Protein   2.3 g

Conclusion

Indeed, camping is a great family activity because you can have time outside and still feel like you're home. Ever since the dawn of humanity, people have been preparing and dining outdoors. But we became more sophisticated somewhere along the line with how we cooked our food, replacing survival-mode hunting and collecting for something a little more fun. Camp cooking today can be as basic or complicated as you choose, depending on your budget and how you camp. Then there's the food itself. Camp cooking can be as easy as grilling hotdogs or something as complicated as preparing a five-course repast using fresh herbs and citrus fruits (but remember to pack a knife and cutting board). Don't forget to truly enhance the meal's enjoyment by adding a cold beverage with fresh ice. This last guide here follows, is essentials designed to help you put together a memorable meal on your camping trip.

The Kitchen

It's not a requirement to buy a full kitchen set for camping. That said, if you do have a kitchen, it's a good idea to pack it in a self-contained set-up. That means you don't have to worry about taking along separate pots and pans, dirty ones, which should never be used at home again. You can also set-up a good kitchen, of course, and buy a separate ice chest to store your perishables, such as meat, cheese, and fruit.

Cookware

You don't need a lot to cook breakfast on a camping trip. A frying pan, Dutch oven, a set of knives, forks, and spoons will be more than enough. If you're worried about cleanliness, consider investing in a cast-iron skillet. It will give the best results, and it's easy to clean.

Camping cookware is not expensive; you can find all sorts of it in stores like Walmart, Target, or Target. When you set up your campsite, set up your cook area too, and you should pay attention to these things:

- Space efficiency. You'll need a work surface big enough for preparing food, and the pots and pans.
- Sturdiness. You'll want your equipment to be solid and sturdy; you'll be working over an open flame, so you don't want the pots and pans to fall over, or more importantly, to burn the leaves or soil.
- Ease of cleaning. You could be spending a lot of time after the main meal cleaning up. Some camping cookware is easier to clean than others.
- Fuel efficiency. You'll need to make sure you have a safe place for your stove. You'll also want your cookware to be easy to pack and fuel-efficient.

The best choice is an enameled Dutch oven. It looks like a regular pot, but it's lighter in weight and can stand up to the high heat a campfire can give off. You can make soups and stews in them, but you can also boil water for making coffee or tea. Dutch ovens can be expensive, though, so you'll want to ensure it will last forever, at least for your camping trips. You can also consider a cast-iron skillet, but it's heavy, so it's really better for car camping. If you're concerned about damage to your skillet, consider a handy dandy skillet guard.

Stoves

As mentioned, you'll need a stove to cook on a camping trip. You may have your own stove at home, but many camp stoves use propane, which you'll need to buy. Another big difference is the firebox's size; your stove should have at least one full side. Most camp stoves will require at least one burner. It gives you more than one way to cook, whether your meal is more elaborate, like a whole chicken, or simpler, like boiling water.

These essentials are needed, but not all are required, depending on the type of camping trip you're going on. A gas-operated stove is also nice to use because not only will it be easier to light, but it may also be heavier and harder to move around and easier to use in an emergency. A stove is not necessary for most people because you don't usually require one while camping, but if you feel you need one or if you're on a road trip, then one will come in handy. It is just about all you need to start.

We hope that this cookbook not only gives you food for thought but also helps start your appetite for food. After all, it's one of the most popular forms of camp cooking today. Never get bored and hungry on your camping trips ever again.